On Target English

Sentence and Word Skills

Year 5

Hilary Frost

Sarah Lindsay

Heather Painter

Edinburgh Gate
Harlow, Essex

Contents

		Sentence	Word	Handwriting
Unit 12 Hide and Seek	page 39	pronoun function commas in sentences	same letters, different sounds – *ough* words antonyms in phrases	*ough* pattern
Unit 13 Tikkatoo's Journey	page 42	types of nouns – common, proper using pronouns	pronoun spelling patterns *en, on* endings	*ould, our* patterns
Unit 14 Diwali	page 45	types of nouns – collective, abstract punctuation practice	letter doubling with suffixes adverbs in speech with *ly*	*dd, ll, tt* patterns
Unit 15 The Lion and Albert	page 48	noun, verb agreement apostrophes for contractions	prefixes to make antonyms using dictionaries	*un, in, im* patterns
Unit 16 Clashes at Oldbury	page 52	adaptation for an audience clauses	*ie, ei* rules using *did* and *done*	*ie, ei* patterns
Unit 17 Zlata's Diary	page 55	prepositions apostrophes for possession	*e* + suffixes initials and acronyms	using capitals
Unit 18 The Man Who Planted Trees	page 58	prepositions conjunctions	*y* to *i* + suffix using *fell, drove, ran*	letter spacing
Unit 19 The Train to Glasgow	page 61	double negatives plural possessive nouns	silent letters using *there, their, there's* and *theirs*	*ere, eir* patterns
Unit 20 Morag and the Monster	page 64	prepositions practising punctuation	dictionary practice using *who* and *whom*	*wha, whe, whi, who, why* patterns
Unit 21 Stop the Airport!	page 67	using the simple present tense writing formal letters	changing verbs to nouns using *doesn't* and *don't*	*ness, ment* patterns
Unit 22 Almaz	page 70	parts of speech practising dialogue	changing nouns to verbs idioms	*ion, sion, tion* patterns

3

A Narrow Squeak

Sentence work

- To discover which words are important

Tip

Sometimes a pronoun, like she, takes the place of a noun.

Remember

Your **mini** sentences will need at least one noun or pronoun and one verb.

Sentence work

- To introduce reported speech

Essential words

> This is a short sentence: *Ethel smiles to herself.*
>
> A sentence needs at least one noun (**Ethel**), and at least one verb (**smiles**), to tell the reader what is happening.

1 Copy these sentences. Underline the nouns in red and the verbs in blue.

    a *The mouse squeaked.*   **b** *Ethel spoke sharply.*

    c *Hedley fetched some food.*   **d** *The cat watched.*

2 Copy these longer sentences. Underline the nouns in red and the verbs in blue, then neatly cross out the words that are not absolutely essential. Make each sentence as short as possible.

    a *The ~~little, fat, furry~~ mouse squeaked ~~noisily to make her friend hear her~~.*

      The mouse squeaked.

    b *The fluffy white cat watched as the mice ran about.*

    c *The little mouse looked up at the hungry-looking white cat.*

    d *In a flash the little mouse ran hurriedly back into the hole.*

    e *The mice all peeped out from the safety of their hole.*

    f *The cat, now feeling even hungrier, licked her lips and smiled at the idea of such a mousy meal.*

Reported speech

> This is called **direct speech**:
>
> *"Do you realise," said Ethel, "that tomorrow is our Silver Wedding Day?"*
>
> This is called **reported speech**:
>
> *Ethel told Hedley that tomorrow would be their Silver Wedding Day.*
>
> **Reported speech** tells us what has been said without using the exact words or speech marks.

1 Copy just the reported speech sentences in this group:

Hedley told Ethel that it only seemed like yesterday that they had been married.

"Well it isn't," said Ethel sharply.

She said he only had to look at her to see that it wasn't.

"You have certainly grown," he said tactfully.

2 Write these direct speech sentences as reported speech. The first is done to help you.

  a "Don't you know why I'm blown out like a balloon?" snapped Ethel at Hedley.

  Ethel asked Hedley if he didn't know why she was blown out like a balloon.

  b "You are going to be a father," she told him.

  c "I'm starving hungry, so fetch me something nice to eat," she told him.

  d "Yes, my dear," he said in amazement. "Anything you fancy!"

Double letters

Letters following the letter *a*, when it makes a short sound at the beginning of a word, are often doubled.

anniversary   attack

1 Copy the words in the box that have a short *a* sound.

allow are appear allergy arch anniversary always arrest arrive armour assembly attack

2 Use a dictionary to help you make a list of words that begin with *a* followed by a double consonant.

Tip

Direct speech is usually in the **present** tense, but reported speech is usually in the **past** tense.

Word work

● To practise some double letter spelling patterns that follow *a*

Tip

a in *a*llow is a *short* sound. It is different from *a* in *a*pe or *a*rmy.

Word work

● To use adverbs to improve spoken sentences

Tip

Most **how** adverbs end with **ly**.

Remember

Speech sentences need speech marks!

Using adverbs in speech

Adverbs can tell us how words are spoken. They give more detail about how things are said:

"Well it isn't," said Ethel <u>sharply</u>.
"You have certainly grown," he said <u>tactfully</u>.

1 Copy these speech verbs, and after each write some **ly** adverbs that could be used with it:

called   loudly excitedly crossly

asked whispered sobbed laughed explained growled

2 Choose two of the verbs in question 1.
Write a speech sentence for each verb, and use adverbs to make the sentences more interesting to read.

Handwriting

al and *all* patterns

al all al all al all al all al all al all al all al all

1 **a** Practise the letter patterns three times.

b Neatly copy these words twice each:

altogether almost already although
alligator allergy allow alley

2 **a** Neatly copy the silly sentence:

Alfie, the aloof alligator, almost always allowed all other alligators along his alley.

b Make your own sentence using *al* and *all* words.

Trip to a Victorian School

Double negatives

- To avoid using double negatives in sentences

If there are two negative words in one sentence, they can sometimes cancel each other out.
A negative sentence then becomes positive:

I won't have no talking in here!

Think about it. This means the teacher **will** allow talking!

1 Correct each of these negative sentences, so that they mean what the writer really intended.

a *Mum didn't have no spare bread for my lunch.*
Mum didn't have any spare bread for my lunch.

b *I couldn't not come yesterday, because I had to help Mum pea-picking at the farm.*

c *The farmer didn't give me nothing for all the extra peas I picked.*

d *No way did I eat none of the peas, even though he said I did!*

e *My sister hasn't got no shoes for school.*

2 Write these sentences, putting *anything* or *nothing* in the gaps:

a *She couldn't see _____ on the blackboard from the back of the room.*

b *There was _____ the teacher could do to help.*

c *If Victorian parents had _____ spare it was needed to buy clothes or food, not glasses.*

 Remember

Negative words are words like no, not, nothing, never, won't, can't, wouldn't.

Sentence work

- To revise key sentence punctuation

Remember

Statement sentences end with a full stop, questions with a ? and exclamations with an !

Tip

Look out for the missing commas and apostrophes in the paragraph.

Word work

- To recognise and use some common prefixes

Remember

Prefixes are groups of letters that are put on the front of words.

Tip

Use a dictionary to check your answers to question 1.

Punctuation practice

1 Each of these sentences is a statement, a question or an exclamation. Add the missing capital letters and punctuation marks.

   a on wednesday 9th july we went to the victorian school

   b did you have a good time

   c it was fantastic

   d where is it

   e it is in the old bradbury school which is now a museum

2 Copy this short paragraph, adding all the punctuation marks that have been left out, including the speech marks:

mr maldoon shouted at rob stand up boy when im speaking to you rob was frightened of him bring your ruler chalk rubber book and anything else on your desk and sit here next to me, then ill be able to keep my eye on you

Prefixes

> Prefixes change the meanings of words, and make other words in a word family.
> **Trans** means *across*.
> **Trans**atlantic means across the Atlantic.

1 **a** If *bi* means **two**, what are these?
   bicycle **bi**plane **bi**focals **bi**noculars

   b If *circum* means **around**, what are these?
   the **circum**ference of a circle **circum**navigation of the world

   c If *auto* means **self**, what are these?
   autobiography **auto**graph **auto**matic machine

   d If *tele* means **at a distance**, what are these?
   television **tele**phone **tele**pathy

2 Use your dictionary to help you find more words in each set with the same prefix. Make sure you know what each word means!

Idioms

Idioms are short phrases which really mean something quite different from what might be expected.

Don't worry, his <u>bark</u> is <u>worse</u> than his <u>bite</u>!

● To understand some common idioms

1 Draw a small humorous picture for each of these idioms. Underneath each, write a sentence to say what it really means.

a get into hot water

b once bitten, twice shy

c my lips are sealed

d my dad's a wet blanket

e don't beat about the bush

f under the weather

2 What would Mr Maldoon mean if he said these to his pupils?

a I will not be taken for a ride by you children.

b You, boy, are not up to it.

c Come on Mary, spill the beans.

d It's as plain as the nose on your face.

tele pattern

Handwriting

tele tele tele tele tele tele tele tele tele tele tele

1 **a** Practise the letter pattern three times.

b Neatly copy the words twice each:

telegraph telepathy television telescope
telephoto telethon telepathic telephone

2 **a** Neatly copy the silly sentence:

Telephone Terry and tell her the telethon will be televised on the new television station.

b Write the eight *tele* words in question 1b in alphabetical order.

Stig of the Dump

 Sentence work

- To learn about *auxiliary* verbs

Tip

Auxiliary verbs are sometimes used by themselves.

Special verbs

Most verbs are **action** words, like *hunt, throw, jump.* Sometimes we need to use some small words to help these main verbs. These are called **auxiliary** or **helper verbs**.

They tell *when* something happens:

Stig <u>*is*</u> <u>*hiding*</u>. *Stig* <u>*was*</u> <u>*hiding*</u>.

We use **is** and **was** if we are writing about one person or thing.

We use **are** and **were** with *you* or if we are writing about more than one person or thing:

Stig and Barney <u>*are*</u> <u>*hiding*</u>.

Stig and Barney <u>*were*</u> <u>*hiding*</u>.

1 Copy these sentences, adding the missing helper verbs:

a *Barney _____ amazed.*

b *The fox _____ coming towards them.*

c *Stig and Barney _____ standing very still.*

d *"You _____ supposed to kill that fox!" stormed Barney.*

e *Now the hounds _____ getting closer.*

f *Stig _____ watching the hound.*

g *The hound _____ afraid of him!*

2 Fill each gap with *There is* or *There are*:

a *_____ many children who enjoy Stig of the Dump.*

b *_____ probably a copy in your library.*

c *_____ lots of children waiting to read it.*

d *_____ a good ending to the story.*

Using commas

> **Commas** are used in lists and with speech marks.
> They are also important to tell a reader when to make a short pause in a sentence.
>
> *He got slowly to his feet, gripping his spear.*

1 Put a comma in each of these sentences:

   a *Come on now's your chance.*

   b *The hound took a step forward making horrible noises in his throat.*

   c *Barney sat at the back of the little cave holding his middle.*

2 Write two sentences about Stig and Barney that need commas.

Some soft and hard *g* patterns

> *The fox gave Stig a glance then plunged into the hole.*
> The letter *g* is usually a **hard** sound, as in Stig.
> But often, especially when it comes before an *e*, it sounds like *j* in jam, as in plunged.

1 a Sort these words into their correct columns:

*garage   grime   cabbage   Stig   damage   bag   package
grinned   cage   page   game   rage   advantage   agent*

soft g words	hard g words

   b Write a sentence explaining what you notice about all the soft *g* words in the column.

2 a Collect words for each of these spelling patterns:

   words beginning with **ge**

   words beginning with **gi**

   b Write a sentence about what difference you notice between the two columns.

Sentence work

● To practise using commas for natural pauses

Word work

● To practise some soft *g* patterns

Tip

A dictionary will help you with some of this work.

Word work

- To learn more contractions

Tip

Beware! Sometimes letters change, too. In question 1, *will not* and *shall not* are tricky!

Contractions

Remember, a **contraction** is made by leaving out some letters and putting an **apostrophe** (') in their place:

"Come on, <u>now's</u> your chance."

now's is a contraction for **now is**.
The **apostrophe** shows where *i* has been left out.

1 Write a contraction for each of these:

that is   there is   was not   we are   would not
has not   here is   they are   will not   shall not   cannot

2 Put a contraction for the words underlined:

a <u>It is</u> coming this way.

b <u>You are</u> supposed to kill it.

c <u>There is</u> no point in hunting unless <u>you are</u> ready to throw your spear!

d <u>I am</u> sure <u>he is</u> laughing at us.

e <u>It will</u> be sorry if it comes out of its hole again!

Handwriting

nge pattern

nge nge nge nge nge nge nge nge nge nge nge nge

1 a Practise the letter pattern three times.

b Neatly copy the words twice each:

hinge fringe range strange
challenge revenge scavenge

2 a Neatly copy the silly sentence:

Mr Vange, a strange man with an orange fringe, arranged the annual sponge throwing challenge.

b Make your own sentence using *nge* words.

Designing a Paddle Boat

Moving words in a sentence

> About a hundred years ago, paddle boats used to travel up and down the Mississippi River in the USA.

Words in a sentence can often be written in a different order, like this:

> Paddle boats used to travel up and down the Mississippi River in the USA, about a hundred years ago.

or

> In the USA about a hundred years ago, paddle boats used to travel up and down the Mississippi River.

 Remember

The writer needs to decide on the best order for the words being written.

1 Write each of these sentences, putting the words in a different order:

a The Mississippi, one of the world's biggest rivers, can sometimes flood and cause huge damage to the towns and villages nearby.

b For many years the steamers would be the best way to travel or send cargo along the huge river.

c Often, especially in the southern states of the USA, the paddle boats would carry jazz bands to entertain the passengers.

 Tip

You may need to add commas where there are short pauses in the sentences.

2 Write this sentence in as many different ways as you can by changing the order of the words:

Slowly the boat would push its way upstream.

Sentence work

- To write clear, accurate instructions

Remember

Writing in the **present** tense means writing as if it is happening now.

Word work

- To practise making plurals of nouns by adding *s* or *es*

Tip

Beware! There is a trick in question 2.

Writing instructions

When writing instructions we normally use short sentences and write in the present tense:

Keep your design simple. Try out models with different widths and lengths.

1 Write each of these sentences in a shorter form:

a When you have finished making your model you could if you wish paint it all sorts of bright colours.

b It is best not to try to paint complicated designs on your model as they usually look rather messy.

c Whatever you do, don't try out your boat until the paint is thoroughly dry or all your work will be spoiled.

2 Write these instruction sentences in the present tense, and leave out unnecessary words:

a He collected together all the tools and materials he needed.
Collect together the tools and materials.

b First he drew a diagram to show how the model might work.

c He cut around the shapes and then carefully smoothed them with sandpaper.

Plural spelling rules

Remember, to make a noun **plural** we usually just **add s**, but, if the noun ends with *s*, *x*, *ch* or *sh* we **add es**:
box box*es*   splash splash*es*

1 Make each of these singular nouns plural:
boat   container   brush   paint   watch   fox   church

2 Make each of these plural nouns singular:
scissors   hutches   flashes   boxes   benches   tables

Synonyms and antonyms

> **Synonyms** are words with a similar meaning:
>
> *big   large*
>
> **Antonyms** are words that have opposite meanings:
>
> *big   small*

● To find and compare antonyms and synonyms

1 Copy these words. Next to each write a synonym and an antonym.

loud   noisy quiet

heavy close difficult dirty

2 Copy these sets of words. Underline each synonym and draw a neat circle around the antonym.

a *break – (mend) lose drop smash*

b *happy – funny unhappy clever cheerful*

c *careful – careless difficult cautious silly*

d *help – make open assist hinder*

e *build – construct tools bricks destroy*

f *kind – unkind sore jealous considerate*

shes and *ches* patterns

> *shes ches shes ches shes ches shes ches shes ches*

1 a Practise the letter patterns three times.

  b Neatly copy the words twice each:

clashes flashes crashes smashes splashes
catches hatches patches scratches matches

2 a Make a list of other words ending with **shes** and **ches**.

  b Make up a sentence using as many **shes** and **ches** words as you can.

The Wind in the Willows

Sentence work

● To edit clumsy sentences

Editing

Whenever we write, it is important to read back what we have written and to look for mistakes.

Sometimes sentences might be clumsy and need changing.

He jumped over the side of the boat into the river the idea of which was to give the boat that he had been sitting in a quick shove to get it going.

He jumped over the side to give the boat a quick shove into the main stream.

1 Rewrite these clumsy sentences, leaving out some words and phrases and changing others:

   a Mole and Rat finished up having a rather silly and foolish argument over who was better at rowing Mole or Rat.

   b In the end the result was that Mole was absolutely bound to fall head first into the cold water which is exactly what happened.

   c You can just imagine the surprise that was felt by the silly Mole when after he had fallen into the cold, very cold water, and had come up spluttering he was dragged out by Rat.

2 These sentences have some spelling mistakes, and also use **got**, **good** and **nice**. Correct the spelling mistakes and think of better words to replace the words underlined.

It wos a <u>nice</u> day wen thay desided to go on the river. It will be <u>good</u> fun, they had said to each uther. But ones they <u>got</u> <u>to</u> the river the argueing startd. It's dificult to think that thay are realy <u>good</u> frends when you see them lick that.

Helpful words

pleasant sunny
great reached
arrived at close

Tenses

> *I rowed   we jumped*
>
> These verbs are in the past tense. We can also write about things in the past in other ways.
>
> Sometimes we use **was** or **were**, and *ing*, when we are writing about the past:
>
> *I was rowing   we were jumping*
>
> At other times we use **had** or **have**:
>
> *I had rowed   we have jumped*
>
> The past tense is the most important tense when we are writing stories.

1 List the three ways you might write the past tense for each of these **family** verbs if **you** had done something:

  a *shout   I shouted   I was shouting   I had shouted*

  b *jump*

  c *talk*

  d *scratch*

  e *swim*

2 Write three sentences about Mole and Rat that includes:

they were sculling

they had fallen in

they swam

Sentence work

- To learn the three main forms of the past tense

Remember

Verb tenses tell us **when** something happened. **Past tense** verbs mean something has happened in the past.

Tip

Beware! There is no such verb as **swimmed**!

17

Word work

- To practise *qu* spellings

qu spelling pattern

The letter **q** never appears alone in English words.
It is always followed by **u**:

squirrel

quack

1 Write a **qu** word to match each picture.

a

b

c

d

Helpful words

question square
squirrel queen

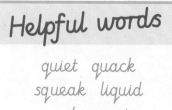

2 Solve this **qu** puzzle. The letters of each word are jumbled.

a A puzzle game. (uizq)

b The noise a mouse makes. (qsuaek)

c Another name for a fluid. (dilqiu)

d The noise a duck makes. (kcuqa)

e Half of a half. (treuqra)

f Not to make a noise. (itque)

Helpful words

quiet quack
squeak liquid
quarter quiz

Roots, prefixes and suffixes

> The **root word** is a basic word. We add **prefixes** and **suffixes** to a root word to make other *family* words.
>
> *How bright and <u>welcome</u> the sun looked.*
>
> <u>welcome</u> <u>unwelcome</u> <u>welcomed</u> <u>welcoming</u>

1 Write the root word for each of these words:

jealously stronger easily jumping suddenly surprisingly grabbed evidently

2 Draw and finish the webs for these root words:

unhappy

happy

easy

ease

appoint

use

qua and *qui* patterns

> *qua qui qua qui qua qui qua qui qua qui qua qui*

1 a Practise the letter patterns three times.
  b Neatly copy the words twice each:

quit quite quiet quietly quickly quack quaint quality quantity quarter

2 a Write the ten *qu* words in question 1b in alphabetical order.
  b Neatly copy the silly sentence:

Queenie, the quaint squirrel, squeaked, then quickly and quietly squashed the mosquito flat.

An Unexpected Surprise

Sentence work

- To change direct speech into reported speech, and reported speech into direct speech

Tip

Direct speech is usually in the **present** tense, but reported speech is usually in the **past** tense.

Direct and reported speech

This is called **direct speech**:

"Phew! We've made it! I'm not too wet," said Jess.

This is **reported speech**:

Jess said she was pleased that they had made it, and that she wasn't too wet.

Remember, **reported speech** tells us what has been said without using the exact words or speech marks.

1 Write these direct speech sentences as reported speech. The first is done for you.

  a "Well I trod in a puddle and my sock is soaking," said William.

    William said that he had trodden in a puddle and his sock was soaking.

  b "Never mind," remarked Tom, "at least we've found somewhere dry to shelter."

  c "Look over here," said Jess anxiously. "I thought this house was empty."

  d "But someone's been here, and quite recently," pointed out Tom, "because there's bread on the table and it's quite fresh."

2 Write these reported speech sentences as direct speech. The first is done to help you.

  a William heard a thump and wondered what it was.

    "What was that thump?" asked William.

  b Jess said that she could hear voices but she couldn't hear what they were saying.

  c William whispered to the others that he thought they should get out of the old house.

  d Tom said that he thought they should try to see who it was in the house.

Starting new lines

 Sentence work

● To start new lines for alternate speakers, and to place commas before speech marks

Remember, each time the speaker changes in a conversation, we begin a new line, as in a play script:

"I trod in a puddle and my sock is soaking," said William.

"Never mind," remarked Tom, "at least we've found somewhere dry to shelter."

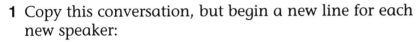

1 Copy this conversation, but begin a new line for each new speaker:

"Look over here," said Jess anxiously. "I thought this house was empty." "Someone's been here quite recently," pointed out Tom, "because there's bread on the table and it's quite fresh." "What was that? I think someone else is here. What shall we do?" asked William.

2 Write these sentences, adding the missing punctuation:

a Dont be such a baby Tom said William

b Hes not a baby said Jess crossly

c Im certainly not a baby added William but I dont want to get caught

d Come on Tom said Jess Lets get out of here

 Remember

Commas, full stops, question marks and exclamation marks come *before* speech marks!

Plurals

 Word work

● To practise plural spelling rules for words ending with *y*

Remember, to make a noun that ends in *y* plural, we usually change the *y* to *i* and then add *es*:

story / stor*ies*

But, if the letter before the *y* is a **vowel**, we just **add *s***:

pla*y* / play*s*

1 Write the plural of each of these nouns:

berry lady activity tray penny day
valley quay bay baby toy puppy

2 Write the plural of each of these nouns:

table puddle bush bread sock play
hobby watch sheep glass fly house

 Tip

Beware! There are tricks in question 2. Think carefully about each one.

Word work

● To build compound words from shorter words

Building compound words

Compound words are words that are made from two shorter words joined together:

passage + way = passageway

1 Copy these words and next to each one write the two smaller words from which it is made:

bedroom crossword farmhouse fingerprint football lipstick lampshade manhole spotlight

Helpful words

one body where
time thing day
how way what

2 Write as many compound words as you can that start with each of these words:

some every

Handwriting

Practising capitals without curves

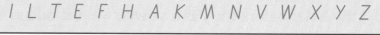

I L T E F H A K M N V W X Y Z

1 Neatly copy the capital letters in the box. None of them has a curve.

2 a Copy these sentences:

LET TIM TELL WILLIAM.
LET HIM TELL WILLIAM.
WILL HE TELL WILLIAM THE TALE?

b Write five words in capital letters, using only the letters in the box.

Picture Poems

Adjectives

Sentence work

- To select adjectives thoughtfully

> **Adjectives** describe nouns.
> Usually we use one adjective to describe a noun:
>
> *pink foxgloves*
>
> Sometimes it is important to add more detail, so we need more adjectives:
>
> *tall, pink, pretty foxgloves*

1 Write three adjectives to describe each of these nouns:
a tree a dog a swimming pool a house

2 **a** Look at the poem *Development* by Robert Froman on page 25. Copy the adjectives he uses to describe the street.

b Make a list of adjectives that might be used to describe the street or road where you live.

Punctuation in poetry

Sentence work

- To consider how commas are used in poetry

> **Commas** are used in sentences to tell the reader when to make a short pause. It is the same in poems.
>
> Commas often come at the end of a line:

To begin,
  jump in
Second step,
  belly flop
Now you're older,
  getting bolder

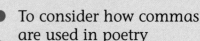
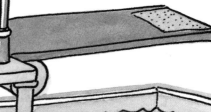

1 Here is a verse from *A Hibernating Hedgehog* by Martin Honeysett. Copy it neatly and add the missing commas and a full stop, where you think they should be.

A hibernating hedgehog
Woke up to greet the spring
He'd set the alarm for half-past May
But he hadn't heard it ring

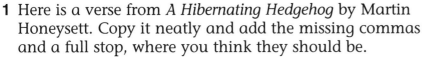

2 Find and copy a verse from a poem of your own choice, looking carefully at how punctuation is used by the poet.

Word work

- To practise plural spelling rules for words ending with *f* or *fe*

Tip

The only important exceptions to the *ves* rule are roofs, chiefs, beliefs and handkerchiefs.

Plurals

Remember, to make plural forms of nouns we normally just add *s* or *es*:

funnel funnel<u>s</u>   box box<u>es</u>

If a word ends in *f* or *fe* it can be tricky!

We *usually* change the *f* or *fe* to *v* and add *es*:

wolf wol<u>ves</u>   wife wi<u>ves</u>

But sometimes we just add *s*:

roof roof<u>s</u>   chief chief<u>s</u>   belief belief<u>s</u>

1 Copy these lists. Join the singular and plural forms of the nouns with a line.

knife	thieves
thief	lives
half	calves
life	wives
leaf	roofs
calf	knives
wife	halves
loaf	loaves
roof	chiefs
chief	leaves

2 Write a short nonsense story about a family of elves, using as many plural words ending in *ves* as you can.

24

Synonyms

Remember, **synonyms** are words or phrases that have the same or a similar meaning.

look: see watch gaze stare observe

Each of these words has a slightly different meaning.

● To consider the differences between synonyms

1 Write at least three synonyms for each of these words. The first is done for you.

lovely *pleasing attractive beautiful delightful*

kind   hungry   happy   sad   exciting

Remember

A **phrase** is a group of words without a verb.

2 Find each of these pairs of words in a dictionary. How does the dictionary suggest that they are different.

a mistake   blunder   **b** noise   uproar

c pleasant   exquisite   **d** weary   exhausted

Tip

A **thesaurus** is useful when you want to find synonyms.

Practising capitals with curves

B C D G J O P Q R S U

1 Neatly copy the capital letters in the box. All of them have a curve.

2 a Neatly copy the poem *Development* below.

b Write five words in capital letters, using only the letters in the box.

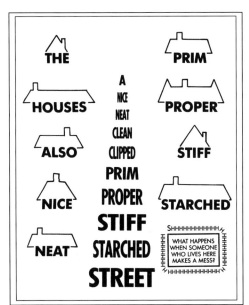

THE   PRIM

HOUSES   A NICE NEAT CLEAN CLIPPED   PROPER

ALSO   STIFF

NICE   PRIM PROPER STIFF STARCHED STREET   STARCHED

NEAT

SHHHHHHHHHHHH
WHAT HAPPENS WHEN SOMEONE WHO LIVES HERE MAKES A MESS?

Robert Froman

Flying Machines

 Sentence work

- To make sure that tenses and subjects agree

Tip

Auxiliary words are sometimes called **helper** verbs.

Auxiliary verbs

Remember, **auxiliary verbs** can tell us *when* something happens.

The plane <u>is</u> flying fast.
The plane <u>was</u> flying fast.

We use **is** and **was** if we are writing about one person or thing.
We use **are** and **were** with **you** or if we are writing about more than one person or thing.

The planes <u>are</u> flying fast.
The planes <u>were</u> flying fast.

1 Copy each of these sentences twice, once in the present tense and once in the past tense. The first one is done for you.

  a *Concorde _____ flying faster than sound.*
    Concorde is flying faster than sound.
    Concorde was flying faster than sound.

  b *The hot-air balloons _____ all different colours.*

  c *A glider _____ soaring in the air currents.*

  d *Two helicopters _____ helping in the rescue.*

  e *The rotors _____ spinning very fast.*

  f *The space shuttle _____ fired high into space.*

  g *Outside, the shuttle _____ getting very hot.*

2 Write these sentences in the plural:

  a *The passenger is climbing into the helicopter.*

  b *A glider was in trouble.*

  c *The red balloon is losing height.*

  d *Each aircraft is different.*

  e *An astronaut is walking on the moon.*

Tip

You might need to change a few words.

Complete sentences

Each **sentence** must make sense to the reader.
To do this, it needs at least one noun (or pronoun) and one verb.
It should begin with a capital letter and end with a full stop.

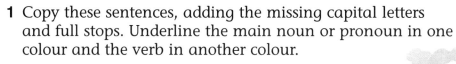

The aircraft flew non-stop to Australia.

capital letter   *full stop*

main noun   *verb*

1 Copy these sentences, adding the missing capital letters and full stops. Underline the main noun or pronoun in one colour and the verb in another colour.

  a the plane crashed into the sea
  b the passengers climbed out safely
  c a helicopter rushed to the scene
  d it soon rescued everyone
  e they were taken back to the airport

Remember

A pronoun stands in place of a noun e.g. *it they she I*

2 These groups of words don't make sense. Add more words and punctuation to make them into sentences so that they **do** make sense.

  a the pilot soon
  b an old lady with a walking stick
  c the thick, dark clouds

The *ful* suffix

Planes have very powerful engines.

If something is **full** of power, we say it is power**ful**.
When used as a suffix, **full** becomes **ful**, and has only one *l*.

Word work

- To recognise that *full* becomes *ful* when used as a suffix

1 Add a *ful* suffix to make each of these words into adjectives, then write each in a short sentence:

  care   wonder   deceit   thought

Tip

By adding **ful** to a word it is made into an adjective, used to describe nouns.

2 Change each of these words into *ful* adjectives. If the root word ends in *y*, first change the *y* to *i*.

  beauty   shame   spite   pity   fancy   sorrow   mercy   hope

Word work

● To practise using a dictionary

Technical terms

When we read about new subjects we sometimes find **technical words** we don't understand, e.g. *thermal*.
This is when dictionaries are very useful.

> **thermal** *n.* the warm, rising air that allows gliders and birds to get lift.

1 Look up these words in a dictionary. Copy the definitions into your book.

rotor   gravity   orbit   altitude   radar

2 Use the information you have found in question 1 to write a simple explanation of each word that a younger child might be able to understand.

Handwriting

ful and *fully* patterns

> ful fully ful fully ful fully ful fully

1 a Neatly copy the letter patterns in the box three times.

  b Copy these words, adding the suffixes *ful* and *fully* to each one. Like this:

  care careful carefully
  shame grace hope wonder pain thought

2 a Neatly copy the silly sentence:

  Bully, the beautiful bull, stopped the spiteful boy.

  b Make your own sentence using *ful* and *fully* words.

How the Ostrich Got His Long Neck

Writing for an audience

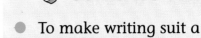
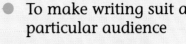

Sentence work

● To make writing suit a particular audience

When we write, we should be thinking of our readers – what they like to read and how well they can understand what we write.

If we write for younger children we need to use shorter sentences and fewer difficult words.

1 Copy this paragraph from *How the Ostrich Got His Long Neck*. Underline any words that a young child might not understand or be able to read.

> He did not dare leave the precious eggs but every time he heard her foolish giggles he strained and stretched his neck, trying to see what was going on. At last the long, tedious night came to an end. As it did so, his wife appeared out of the grey distance to take over her duties once more.

Tip

Make sure that there are no confusing phrases, like *take over her duties once more.*

2 Now write the paragraph again using words and shorter sentences that might more easily be read and understood by a young child.

Sentence work

- To learn about how pauses are shown

Punctuation for pauses

There are three types of punctuation mark that are used inside sentences that mean the reader should take a small pause. They are the comma, semicolon and dash (, ; –), printed in red in the sentences below. ; and – mean a slightly longer pause than a comma.

> He tried to shake it back to its former length, but no matter what he did, it just stayed the same; he had stretched it beyond return.
>
> And that is why the ostrich has a long neck – a lasting memory of a flighty wife.

1 Put a semicolon in these sentences where you think it would help to have a longer pause than a comma:

a He was deeply upset more upset than he believed possible.

b The ostrich now had a long neck a neck longer than any other bird he knew.

c He felt totally let down never had he felt so let down in his life.

2 Look through a reading book to find a sentence with a semicolon or dash. Copy it into your book.

Word work

- To practise soft *c* spellings and find frequent patterns

Soft *c*

> Mr Ostrich decided to look after the eggs.

The letter *c* can often sound like an *s*. We then say it has a **soft** sound.

1 Copy these soft *c* words into two lists, depending on the letter that comes after the *c*.

certain city cement cinema centre cigar pencil celery decide century ferocity process citizen December acid excellent

2 Copy these words. Say them quietly to yourself and write a sentence on what you notice about the sounds made by the letter *c*s.

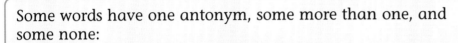
certificate success civic circuit
circle electricity cyclone cycle

Thinking about antonyms

Some words have one antonym, some more than one, and some none:

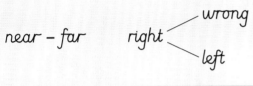
near – far   right ⟨ wrong / left ⟩   green

1 Sort the words in the box into their correct columns.

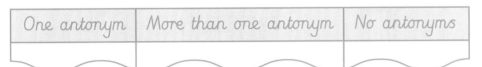
long small ostrich absent black ugly clear go safe wall

One antonym	More than one antonym	No antonyms

2 a Add more words of your own to each column.
 b Write a sentence to explain why some words have antonyms and others have no antonyms.

ance, *ence* and *ince* patterns

ance ence ince ance ence ince ance ence ince

1 a Practise the letter patterns three times.
 b Neatly copy the words twice each:

mince since prince
distance entrance importance
sentence silence violence

2 Add *ance*, *ence* or *ince* to make complete words:

ch_____ w_____ f_____ tr_____ evid_____
assist_____ obedi_____ conv_____

Word work

- To find out how some words have one antonym, some more than one, and some none

Remember

Antonyms are opposites.

Handwriting

Tip

Use a dictionary to help you.

How Sound Works

Sentence work

● To learn how sentences can be reordered

Changing sentences

Some sentences can be changed around, altering just a few words, so that they have a different meaning:

When a stick is banged on a drum, the skin vibrates.

The drum skin vibrates when a stick is banged on it.

Does the skin vibrate when a stick is banged on a drum?

1 Change these statements into questions. You might need to alter one or two words. The first is done for you.

   a *The man is banging the drum too hard.*

   Is the man banging the drum too hard?

   b *I can hear better through my left ear.*

   c *Yes, that boy plays the drum very well.*

   d *The concert is next week in the school hall.*

2 Write each of these sentences in **three** different ways. One should be a question. Change as few words as possible.

   a *The vibrating drum makes the air next to it vibrate.*

   b *Other instruments, not only the drum, make the air vibrate.*

   c *My favourite instrument, by far, is the drum.*

   d *According to my teacher, I expect to be ready for my drum exam by next month.*

Capital letters and full stops

1 All of the capital letters and punctuation marks have been left out of these sentences. Copy them and correct them.

  a my brother rupert is learning to play the recorder

  b uncle jim our favourite uncle says he is doing well

  c will you come and hear me when i play in the concert

  d when is the concert

  e it is on Tuesday next week at bungbury town hall

2 Write this paragraph, putting in the speech marks as well as the other punctuation and capital letters:

i certainly enjoyed that said uncle jim as we drove home so did I added mum we all felt very proud what was the tune called rupert asked uncle jim it was a jazzed up version of the teddy bears picnic I said well it didnt sound a bit like that he laughed

Sentence work

● To revise using capital letters and full stops

Tip

Look out for the missing commas.

Remember

Start a new line each time the speaker changes.

Word work

- To show how letter patterns don't always make the same sounds

Tip

This spelling pattern is sometimes called a **magic e** pattern.

Helpful words

bone one glove
dove rope move

Helpful words

phone dove shove prove
above lose shone done
one glove come gone
move some none love

Word work

- To recognise *sound* words

Same letters, different sounds

> They m*ove* like waves and c*ome* back.

The same letter pattern (**o-e**) makes a different sound in these two words.

1 Write a word that rhymes with each of these words. The pictures will give you a clue.

shove   love

done   prove

phone   hope

2 Copy this table. Add as many **o-e** words as you can in each section.

o says o as in hot	gone
o says u as in sun	some
o says oo as in spoon	move
o says its own name	rope

Onomatopoeia

Onomatopoeia is a Greek word that means *word making*. **Onomatopoeic** words are *sound* words, like bang, crunch and cuckoo.

1 Sort the words in the box into two columns. Some words you might choose to put in both columns.

> clang patter pitter rustling ping hum
> tinkle twang sprinkles splishes bang
> rumble whistle strum drip thump crash

Music sound words	Weather sound words

2 In this extract from her poem about rain, Eve Merriman makes up some onomatopoeic words:

> *Spack a spack speck flick a flack fleck*
> *Freckling the window pane.*

Make up or think of onomatopoeic words to describe:

a sounds on a beach

b sounds in autumn

c a young baby

d church bells ringing

ove and *oving* patterns

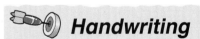 **Handwriting**

> ove oving ove oving ove oving ove oving

1 a Practise the letter patterns three times.

 b Neatly copy the words twice each:

> dove love glove shove above move prove

2 a Copy these words, and add *ing* to each one:

> love loving
> shove move prove

 b Make a silly sentence using ***ove*** and ***oving*** words.

The Importance of Trees

Sentence work

- To make sure nouns and verbs match and are either both plural or both singular

Tip

Don't forget, plural nouns need plural verbs and singular nouns need singular verbs.

Remember

Pronouns, words like **I**, **it** and **we**, are used in place of nouns.

Matching nouns and verbs

Remember, we usually add *s* or *es* to make a noun **plural**, but we usually add *s* or *es* to make a verb **singular**!

the tree<u>s</u> grow tall
   noun   verb

a tree grow<u>s</u> tall
   noun   verb

1 Choose the correct verb for each of these sentences.

  a The trees grow/grows tall.

  b A tree grows/grow in the field.

  c A woodcutter fells/fell the old trees.

  d Two woodcutters fell/fells the biggest trees.

  e The boys come/comes to watch.

  f The man tell/tells them to stand well clear.

2 Copy and finish these sentences. Choose a **helper** verb *is* or *are* that matches each noun or pronoun.

  a He _____ afraid the tree might fall near them.

  b They _____ disappointed.

  c The man _____ worried the boys might get hurt.

  d The man _____ right, and they kept right away!

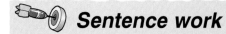
Changing sentences

> Trees are important for many reasons.
>
> For many reasons trees are important.
>
> Both of these sentences use the same words in a different order, but both have the same meaning.

1 Copy each of these. Then write each sentence a second time, using the words in a different order.

   a For birds, trees are a safe haven.

   b Trees are also important for other reasons.

   c The air we breathe would not be the same without the trees of the world.

   d Ornamental trees are found in parks and gardens in cities.

2 Write each of the sentences in question 1 as a question. The first is done for you.

   a How are trees a safe haven for birds?

Sentence work

● To find out how words in sentences can be moved about without changing the meaning

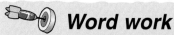

> Helpful words
>
> How   Why
>
> Where

Homophones

> Remember, **homophones** are words that sound the same but are spelt differently and have different meanings.
>
> <u>Would</u> you like to play in the <u>wood</u>?

Word work

● To revise some of the more important homophones

1 Copy these words and next to each one write a homophone. The first one is done to help you.

   meet <u>meat</u> here there wear nose
   new quay hare right by

2 Write sentences to show that you know the meanings of these homophones:

   a rode rowed road

   b rain reign rein

   c through threw

   d tail tale

   e week weak

Word work

● To learn about expressions that compare things

Tip

Similes are expressions that suggest different things are in some ways **similar** to each other.

Special expressions that describe

> A tree is <u>a</u> <u>whole</u> <u>world</u>   <u>a</u> <u>nursery</u> for fledglings
> trees <u>are</u> <u>barricades</u>

Expressions like these, that compare things, are not actually true but can be helpful ways of describing.

1 Choose a word from the box to finish these expressions. They are called similies.

| post | ox | lion | needle | cucumber | fox |

as strong as an _____   as cool as a _____

as cunning as a _____   as brave as a _____

as deaf as a _____   as sharp as a _____

2 Write sentences to explain these expressions.

a tree is a safe haven

as gentle as a dove

the hare ran like the wind

the sky was on fire

 ## *Handwriting*

Using capitals

A B C D E F G H I J K L M N O P Q R S T U V W X Y Z

1 Copy this sign:

KEEP OUT
TRESPASSERS
WILL BE PROSECUTED

2 Design a more friendly notice, asking visitors to the wood to respect the trees and wildlife, and not to leave any litter. Print your sign using capital letters.

Hide and Seek

Pronouns

> <u>Jim</u> thought that <u>Mitzi, Joe and Ali</u> would not find <u>Jim</u> if <u>Jim</u> hid in the shed.
>
> Notice how this clumsy sentence can be made much better by using **pronouns** instead of repeating lots of nouns:
>
> <u>He</u> thought that <u>they</u> would not find <u>him</u> if <u>he</u> hid in the shed.

1 Rewrite these sentences using a pronoun in place of each of the underlined words:

a <u>Jim</u> liked to play with <u>Mitzi, Joe and Ali</u>.

b <u>Mitzi, Joe and Ali</u> played a trick on <u>Jim</u>.

c <u>The trick</u> was an unkind trick that <u>Mitzi, Joe and Ali</u> played on <u>Jim</u>.

d <u>Jim</u> thought he wouldn't play with <u>Mitzi, Joe and Ali</u> again.

2 Sometimes pronouns are part of contractions. Write the pronoun in each of these contractions:

I'm they'll they're I've he's she'll it'll we've

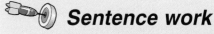

Sentence work

● To use pronouns effectively

Remember

Pronouns are short words we sometimes use in place of nouns.

Helpful words

it they
him them

39

Sentence work

- To practise using commas in longer sentences

Tip

It helps if you read the sentences quietly to yourself to see where the pauses need to come.

Word work

- To show how letter patterns don't always make the same sounds

Helpful words

through trough rough
cough bough borough
fought throughout
bought dough thorough
enough though plough

Using commas in sentences

We put a **comma** where we want our readers to take a short pause in long, complicated sentences:

He hid in the shed, which smelt like the seaside, while he was waiting for the others to find him.

1 Copy these sentences, putting a comma wherever you think the reader should make a short pause:

   a *He tried not to sneeze for if he did the others would hear him.*

   b *Not having won Hide and Seek before Jim was keen that they did not find him.*

   c *Hearing them whisper at the door he held his breath desperately trying not to burst!*

   d *He began to climb out ready to give them a surprise.*

2 We also use commas after **Yes** and **No** at the beginnings of a sentence. Copy these sentences, putting commas wherever they are needed.

   a *No I will not play with you after you were so mean.*

   b *Yes we were unkind but we didn't want to upset you did we Mitzi?*

   c *No we didn't especially as it is your birthday.*

   d *Yes I will play another game but only if you promise not to gang up on me.*

Same letters, different sounds

cough, though, through, rough, bough, borough
The letter pattern **ough** makes several different sounds.

1 Use a dictionary to find the meaning of these words:

   dough doe   through threw
   bough bow   fought fort
   rough ruff   sort sought

2 Make a list of as many words as you can with **ough** in them, and sort them into groups in which the **ough** letter pattern makes the same sound.

Antonyms in phrases

● To revise antonyms (opposites)

> **Hide** and **seek** are antonyms.
> They are used for the name of a game.
>
>

Remember

Antonyms are words that have opposite, or nearly opposite, meanings.

1 Write an antonym for each of these words:

alive	clean	empty	here	kind
love	plural	quiet	old	true

2 Sometimes antonyms are used as expressions in sentences. Write sentences to explain what each expression means.

a blowing hot and cold

b the ups and downs of life

c the ins and outs of the situation

d all this coming and going

ough pattern

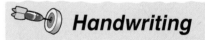
Handwriting

> ough   ough   ough   ough   ough   ough   ough   ough

1 a Practise the letter pattern three times.
   b Neatly copy the words twice each:

> thoughtful roughly coughing ploughed
> throughout thoughtfully coughed ploughing

2 a Neatly copy the silly sentence:

> The ploughman thought he'd ploughed the rough ground enough.

   b Make your own sentence using *ough* words.

Tikkatoo's Journey

Sentence work

● To revise common and proper nouns

Remember

Nouns are **naming** words. **Proper nouns** begin with a capital letter.

Nouns

Sledge and *dog* are **common nouns**. They are the names of things.

Tikkatoo and *Nanook* are **proper nouns**. They are *special* names.

1 a Sort these words into two columns:

iceberg Canada sun sledge grandfather
Tikkatoo Greenland eyes goddess snow seals

Common nouns	Proper nouns

b Write a sentence that uses a noun from each of the lists.

c Copy this sentence. Underline the common nouns in red and the proper nouns in blue.

Tikkatoo's grandfather, Nanook, is ill and he needs a flame from the sun.

2 a Look around. Write five common nouns that you can see.

b Write five proper nouns that are connected with your school.

c Write five proper nouns that are connected with where you live and who you live with.

Using pronouns

> *He she we* are pronouns that are used instead of people's names. These are called **personal pronouns**.
>
> *Hers theirs* are pronouns that are used to show who owns something. These are called **possessive pronouns**.

1 Sort these **personal** and **possessive** pronouns into the table.

> he she hers we his yours them theirs they its I mine

Personal pronouns	Possessive pronouns

2 Next to each of the pronouns is a small letter. Write the name of the person each pronoun stands for.

"Tikkatoo," said Nanook.

"Grandfather," (a) <u>he</u> cried and threw (b) <u>his</u> arms around (c) <u>him</u> and hugged (d) <u>him</u> very tight. There (e) <u>they</u> sat, the light dancing about (f) <u>them</u>. a = Tikkatoo

Tricky pronoun spellings

> These spellings are important because we use them often:
>
> me my mine our ours
> you your yours you're you've you'll
> they they've they'll they're their theirs

1 Complete these sentences using the words above:

a Grandad gave <u>m___</u> a dog. He's <u>m___</u> favourite because he's <u>m___</u>!

b If <u>y___</u> driven dogs, <u>y___</u> know <u>y___</u> need to keep <u>y___</u> eye on the lead dog.

c <u>T___</u> pulled <u>t___</u> sledge up the slope.

2 Copy these pronoun contractions and write out the two words each one stands for:

a they've <u>they have</u>   **b** they'll they're

c you're you've you'll   **d** he'll we're I'm she's

Sentence work

● To practise using pronouns

Word work

● To practise pronoun spellings

> *Helpful words*
>
> **a** mine me my
>
> **b** you your yours
> you're you've you'll
>
> **c** their they theirs

Word work

- To be aware of and practise *en* and *on* endings

en and *on* endings

> The golden box lay open on the cotton cloth.
> Notice that the word endings **en** and **on** sound similar.

1 Write a word ending with **en** or **on** to match each clue:
  a six plus one   **b** a young cat   **c** bad
  d fastens clothes   **e** made of wood   **f** forgive
  g made of gold   **h** meat from sheep   **i** fried for breakfast

2 Write six more words that end with **on**.

Helpful words

rotten wooden golden
kitten seven pardon
mutton button bacon

 Handwriting

ould and *our* patterns

> ould our ould our ould our ould our

1 a Practise the letter patterns three times.
  b Neatly copy the words twice each:

  your yours our ours
  should shouldn't would wouldn't could couldn't

2 a Neatly copy and make up an ending to this sentence:
  I would if I could, and I know I should, come to your ...
  b Make your own sentences using *shouldn't wouldn't couldn't*.

44

Diwali

Nouns

Candle and *classroom* are **common nouns** and *Pushpa* and *Diwali* are **proper nouns**.

Here are two other sorts of nouns.

Team and *crowd* are **collective nouns**. They are names for *collections* of people or things.

Happiness and *belief* are **abstract nouns**, names of ideas and feelings that you can't see, touch or smell.

 Sentence work

● To revise the different types of nouns and recognise abstract nouns

 Remember

Nouns are **naming** words.

1 Which collective noun would you use instead of **lot** in these phrases?

a lot of people   a lot of elephants   a lot of birds

Helpful words

bunch   herd
crowd   flock
swarm   pile

a lot of stones   a lot of flowers   a lot of insects

2 a List five abstract nouns for feelings you sometimes have. Start with:

happiness

b Write the abstract nouns in this group of words:

excitement sorrow Diwali band jealousy
sadness pity envy candle fright

c Write sentences using these abstract nouns:

anger   excitement   curiosity

Sentence work

- To practise using the most important punctuation marks and capital letters

Remember

Proper nouns and **I** always need capital letters.

Remember

Start a new line each time a different person starts to speak.

Word work

- To practise adding suffixes to words ending with a short vowel and single consonant

Punctuation practice

When editing work, check your punctuation carefully. Make sure every sentence begins with a capital letter. Poor punctuation makes even good writing seem bad.

1 Copy these, adding missing punctuation and capital letters:

  a pushpa always enjoys diwali

  b their teacher mrs chopra has just started at blacktown primary school

  c where did mrs chopra teach before

  d the class has made a frieze which shows rama returning to his kingdom surrounded by people holding lighted oil lamps

2 Rewrite this passage correctly, adding the speech marks and commas:

This frieze is excellent said Mrs Chopra enthusiastically. Can we invite the infants to come and see it? asked Mira. Yes I'm sure we can replied her teacher but only if you tidy up the classroom first. We'll do that said Greg who wanted his little brother to see what he had done.

Adding suffixes

jog jogging bat batted big bigger

To add **ing**, **ed** or **er** to a short word, first look at the letter before the last letter.

If it is a single vowel, then double the last letter before adding the suffix.

1 Add ing to these words. Decide whether you need to double the last letter before adding ing.

sit sitting bat slim hop hit fit sell chop cut shop tap let peck swim bat net

2 Write these words in the past tense. Add ed to some, but others will need to be changed in other ways.

drop nod slip sit throw bat slim hop swim fit sell pat

Using adverbs in speech

Remember, adverbs can tell us *how* words are spoken. They give more detail about how things are said. They usually end in **ly**.

"We're performing our play tonight," said Leena, <u>excitedly</u>.

"Yes, but let's not get too excited," said Mrs Chopra, <u>calmly</u> and <u>quietly</u>.

Word work

● To recognise that adverbs often end in *ly*

Helpful words

merrily   rudely
cheerfully   slowly
politely   grumpily
quietly   crossly
sadly   quickly
happily

1 Make adverbs in the same word families as these words:

cross <u>crossly</u>   sad   quick   slow   quiet   cheerful
polite   rude   grumpy   merry   happy

2 Copy these sentences, adding an adverb to fill each gap:

a "Now, I want everyone on their very best behaviour," said Mrs Chopra, _____.

b "Ali's pinched my hat," shouted Jamie, _____.

c "I don't think I'll remember my lines," said Pushpa, _____.

d "Don't worry, you will," said Mrs Chopra, _____.

Tip

If a word ends in *y*, change *y* to *i* before adding *ly*.

dd, *ll* and *tt* patterns

dd ll tt dd ll tt dd ll tt dd ll tt dd ll tt dd ll tt dd ll tt

Handwriting

1 a Practise the letter patterns three times.
b Neatly copy the words twice each:

filling   milling   drilling   grilling
hitting   fitting   knitting   sitting
plodding   nodding   prodding

2 a Neatly copy the silly sentence:

Gran was sitting and nodding as she was grilling her knitting.

b Make your own sentence using *dd*, *ll* and *tt* words.

The Lion and Albert

Sentence work

- To make sure nouns and verbs match and are either both plural or both singular

Tip

Four of the sentences need correcting.

Remember

Was and **were** are verbs.

Tip

We usually add *s* or *es* to make a noun **plural**, but we usually add *s* or *es* to make a verb **singular**!

Matching nouns and verbs

> *A grand little lad was Albert.*
> We use **was** if we are writing about one person or thing.
>
> *The Ramsbottoms were on holiday in Blackpool.*
> *"You were a very wicked lion," said Mum.*
> We use **were** with **you** or if we are writing about **more than one** person or thing.

1 In *The Lion and Albert*, the poet sometimes uses **was** and **were** incorrectly. Some of these are correct, but some are wrong. Copy and correct the wrong sentences.

   a *A grand little lad was young Albert.*

   b *The waves, they was fiddlin' and small.*

   c *There was no wrecks.*

   d *There were one great big Lion called Wallace.*

   e *Now Albert had heard about Lions,*
   How they was ferocious and wild.

   f *The keeper was quite nice about it.*

2 Choose the correct singular or plural verb to match the noun.

   a *Albert like/likes the seaside.*

   b *Albert and his dad swim/swims in the sea.*

   c *Mum, Dad and Albert go/goes to the zoo.*

   d *They see/sees the lions in a cage.*

   e *Albert poke/pokes Wallace, the biggest lion.*

   f *He pull/pulls Albert into the cage.*

   g *The lion eat/eats Albert!*

   h *His parents find/finds the manager to complain.*

Apostrophes for contractions

- To practise using apostrophes for contractions

Remember, a **contraction** is made by leaving out some letters and putting an **apostrophe** (') in their place.

What's to do?

I think it's a shame and a sin.

What's is a contraction for **What is**

it's is a contraction for **it is**.

The **apostrophe** shows where letters have been left out.

Tip

Contract means to get smaller.

When we make a contraction, we **close the space** between the words.

1 Write a contraction for each of these:

it will   has not   do not   you are   she is
would not   cannot   we shall

2 Copy the sentences and put a contraction for the words underlined:

a *There is a famous seaside place called Blackpool.*

b *They did not think much to the ocean.*

c *Mother said, "Right is right."*

d *I think it is a shame.*

e *Someone has got to be summonsed.*

Helpful words

hasn't   wouldn't
it'll   we'll
she's   don't
you're   can't

Word work

- To recognise how prefixes can make negative words

Remember

Antonyms are opposites. Some more **prefixes** are *de*, *en* and *ex*.

Using prefixes to make antonyms

happy   unhappy

We add a prefix to some words to make the antonym.

1 Add a prefix from the box to each of these words to make their antonyms.

| im   in   non   un   il |

lock   convenient   sense   possible   legible
legal   polite   fortunate   reasonable   probable

2 Swap the underlined prefix for another prefix to make the antonyms of these words:

<u>out</u>side   <u>in</u>side   <u>in</u>crease   <u>dis</u>courage
<u>ex</u>ternal   <u>im</u>port   <u>de</u>flate   <u>up</u>stairs

Word work

- To practise using dictionaries

Remember

The **main parts of speech** are nouns, pronouns, adjectives, verbs, adverbs, conjunctions and prepositions.

Using a dictionary

limp (1) *v.* to walk lamely. *n.* **limp** a hobble.
limp (2) *adj.* flabby, drooping.
linen *n.* 1. cloth made of flax fibres. 2. articles
made of this, as *household linen*.
liner *n.* a large passenger ship or aircraft.
linger *v.* to wait behind, to loiter.
liniment *n.* a soothing liquid for rubbing on
bruises.
linnet *n.* a small, brown song-bird.
linseed *n.* flax seed. *n.* **linseed oil** oil from
crushed flax seed.
lion *n.* a wild animal of Africa and
southern Asia (*fem.* **lioness**)
lion-hearted brave.
liquefy *v.* to make liquid.

Dictionaries contain lots of information about each word – how it is spelt, what it means, what part of speech it is and if it has related words or sayings.

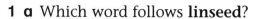

1 a Which word follows **linseed**?

  b How many meanings are there for **limp**?

  c What is a **linnet**?

  d What does **lion-hearted** mean?

  e Write these words with the correct spelling:
  linar   linament   linnit   liquifey

2 a Why are there two entries for **limp**?

  b Is **lion** a noun or a verb? How can you tell?

  c Does **liner** come before or after **linen**? Why?

  d What part of speech is **linger**?

  e These are the next four words which would follow
  liquefy. Write them in the correct order.

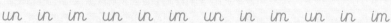

liquor   liquid   liquorice   liquidate

un, *in* and *im* patterns

 **Handwriting**

un in im un in im un in im un in im

1 a Practise the letter patterns three times.

  b Neatly copy the words twice each:

  undo   untrue   untidy
  inside   incorrect   invisible
  impossible   imperfect   impatient

2 a Add the prefix *im* to each of these words.
  What do you notice?

  modest   mature   movable   mobile

  b Write a sentence using two of the new words you
  have made.

Clashes at Oldbury

Sentence work

● To practise writing for a different audience

Tip

Use a thesaurus and a dictionary to help you.

Writing for someone else

> When we write, it is important to think who will be reading what we write. We should write words and sentences that suit those people.
>
> We might write in a **friendly way** for our family, or in a **careful way** if we are giving information, or in an **easy-to-read way** if it is for young children.

Look at this paragraph from the newspaper article:

> **AFTER YEARS OF PROTEST** and arguments, yesterday the diggers moved in. Work on the Oldbury by-pass has begun! But if the road builders had thought their problems were over, they were wrong. There were hundreds of people surrounding Mile Lake, the cause of most of the protest. There was also a group of protesters high up in a tree, where they have built a hut. They are almost impossible for the police to reach.
>
> Even though the road builders have paid biologists and botanists from the university to move the rare toads and almost extinct water anemones out of Mile Lake, the protesters don't believe such sites should be destroyed.

1 Write a synonym for each of these, so that they would be easier for a young child to read and understand:
cause of   almost impossible   biologists
botanists   university   rare   extinct

2 Rewrite the paragraph from the newspaper for young children to be able to read and understand. Use easier words and make some of the long sentences shorter.

Sentence work

● To introduce clauses

Tip

A clause is a section of a sentence, with a verb.

Clauses

> Each sentence can be divided into **clauses**.
> Very short, simple sentences have just one clause, but most sentences have two or more clauses.
> This sentence has one clause:
>
> *Work on the Oldbury by-pass has begun!*
> This sentence has two clauses:
>
> *Protesters were lying down in groups/*
> *to stop the machines from moving.*

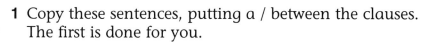

1 Copy these sentences, putting a / between the clauses. The first is done for you.

a *There was also a group of protesters high up in a tree,/ where they have built a hut.*

b *There were hundreds of police officers on duty to prevent the protests.*

c *The traffic was congested in the middle of Oldbury and people were having a problem crossing the road.*

2 Copy each clause. Then add a second clause that could be used to complete each sentence.

a *The town has needed a by-pass <u>because</u> ...*

b *Some people wanted to save the wildlife <u>so</u> ...*

c *The police tried to prevent the protests <u>but</u> ...*

d *The lorries will be better on a by-pass <u>where</u> ...*

ie and *ei*

> *The protesters don't bel<u>ie</u>ve the sites should be destroyed.*
>
> ***i*** comes *before* **e** (when the sound is **ee**): *bel<u>ie</u>ve*
> • *except* after **c**: *rec<u>ei</u>ve c<u>ei</u>ling*
> • *or* when the sound is not **ee**: *r<u>ei</u>gn h<u>ei</u>r for<u>ei</u>gn*

1 a Copy these words into the two columns.

relieve chief niece freight neighbours shriek siege their brief eight weight wield believe grief rein deceit achieve leisure sleight receipt vein shield field receive

Words with the ie pattern	Words with the ei pattern

b Put a coloured dot next to the words with the **ee** sound.

2 Write a sentence to say what you notice about the words with a coloured dot **and** the *ei* spelling pattern.

Tip

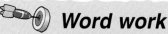

A conjunction has been given to help you.

Word work

● To practise the *i* before *e* rule and its exceptions

Word work

- To learn when to use *did* and when to use *done*

Tip
Sometimes **done** and the helper verb may be separated
e.g. He **had** not **done** his work.

Handwriting

Using did and done

There is an easy way to remember when to use **did** and when to use **done**.
Never use a helping verb with *did*:
The police <u>did</u> their best to keep the peace.
Always use a helping verb with *done*:
The police <u>had</u> <u>done</u> their best to keep the peace.

1 Use the correct verb in these sentences:
  a *The protesters (did/done) their utmost to stop the work.*
  b *Three protesters had (did/done) most of the planning.*
  c *The police have (did/done) lots of planning too.*
  d *The builders (did/done) their best to save the wildlife.*
  e *"They have not (did/done) enough," said one protester.*
  f *"We couldn't have (did/done) more," replied a builder.*

2 Write one sentence using **did** and one sentence using **done**.

ie and *ei* patterns

ie ei ie ei ie ei ie ei ie ei ie ei ie ei

1 **a** Practise the letter patterns three times.
  b Neatly copy the words twice each:

  niece piece brief grief chief thief
  receive deceive eight weight either neither

2 **a** Neatly copy the silly sentence:

  The priests were relieved when the thief returned their eighty handkerchiefs.

  b Make your own sentence using **ie** an **ei** words.

54

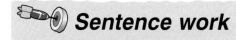
Zlata's Diary

Prepositions

> **Prepositions** tell us where something is, or its **position**:
>
> Zlata lived <u>in</u> Sarajevo.
> We ran <u>into</u> our cellar.

1 Write the preposition in each of these sentences:

   a Zlata went into the hall.

   b The cellar was under the flats.

   c Planes were flying above the buildings.

   d Shells were dropping on the city.

   e Daddy ran to the flat.

Tip

Pre**positions** tell us about **positions** of things!

2 Write sentences about the picture using these prepositional phrases. When you have finished, underline the prepositions.

   a in the road

   b over the fence

   c from the sky

   d near the dustbins

Sentence work

- To practise using apostrophes for possession

Who owns it?

Zlata's diary

Remember, when something belongs to someone we use an apostrophe (') and an *s*, like this: *'s*.

Zlata's is called a **possessive noun**.

For plurals of nouns, like girls, we must put an apostrophe *after* the *s*.

The three girls' diaries.

1 Write these using possessive nouns:

   a the pet canary belonging to Zlata   *Zlata's pet canary*

   b the seed belonging to the canary

   c the office where Dad works

   d the garden belonging to the neighbours

   e the speech by the President

2 Copy each phrase, adding an apostrophe in the correct place:

   a *the two planes bombs*   **b** *the three flats windows*

   c *the four boys game*   **d** *the two girls bags*

   e *the five houses roofs*   **f** *the two boys coats*

Write a sentence using two of the phrases you have written.

Word work

- To learn the spelling rule and some exceptions

Adding suffixes to words ending with *e*

To add a suffix when a word ends with *e*:
drop the *e* if the suffix begins with a *vowel*:

   wake + ing = waking

keep the *e* if the suffix begins with a *consonant*:

   wake + ful = wakeful

1 a Add *ing* to: *take make drive slope hope*
  b Add *able* to: *use value believe cure recognise*

2 a Add *ly* to: *close like fine wise brave*
  b Add *ful* to: *grace hope shame care waste*

Remember

The vowels are *a e i o u*.
Sometimes *y* counts as a vowel, too.

Be careful! Most spelling rules have exceptions, like:
true/truly, argue/argument

Making long words shorter!

Sometimes two words are made into one as a **contraction**.
There are other ways we sometimes abbreviate:
  1 By leaving off prefixes or suffixes: (aero)plane
  2 By using initials: NATO (**N**orth **A**tlantic **T**reaty **O**rganisation)

Word work

● To learn about abbreviations

Tip

Abbreviate means to shorten.
When initial letters make a word, it is called an **acronym**.

1 Find out what these initials stand for:
  EU RAF UN www OXFAM RSPCA FC BBC

2 Write down what these words are often abbreviated to:
  telephone omnibus photograph hippopotamus

Using capitals

Handwriting

A B C D E F G H I J K L M N O P Q R S T U V W X Y Z

1 Copy this sign:

RSPB RESERVE
PLEASE DON'T
DISTURB NESTING
BIRDS

2 Make a list of as many countries and organisations as you can that we know by their initials.

The Man Who Planted Trees

Prepositions

> Prepositions tell us the **position** of something compared with something else:
>
> *The man went walking <u>in</u> a desolate place.*

1 Look through some reading books, and list as many prepositions as you can find.

2 Copy these sentences. The preposition has been left out. Write each of the sentences three times, using a different preposition each time.

   a He emptied a pile of acorns _____ the table.

   b The shepherd went _____ the hills.

   c He planted the acorns _____ the rocks.

Helpful words

next to	against
through	behind
between	towards
onto	very near

Tip

Notice how the meaning of the sentences changes.

Sentence work

● To revise when and how to join sentences

Sentences – long or short?

> In *The Man Who Planted Trees,* Jean Giono sometimes writes short, brief sentences:
>
> I smoked my pipe. I offered to help. He said he had to do it himself.
>
> and sometimes he writes longer sentences:
>
> When he reached the place he was aiming for, he began to make holes in the ground with his rod, putting an acorn in each and then covering it up again.

1 Join each of these pairs of sentences with conjunctions to make single sentences:

  a I offered to help. He said he had to do it himself.

  b He was concentrating hard. We had no conversation.

  c The old man collected a large heap of acorns. He divided them into ten groups.

  d He examined them minutely. He wanted only those that were perfect.

2 Divide these long, single sentences to make shorter sentences. You will need to change a few words.

  a When he reached the place he was aiming for, he began to make holes in the ground with his rod, putting an acorn in each and then covering it up again.

  b I asked the old shepherd if this land was his but he said it wasn't, and he didn't know who the owner was though he thought it might be common land.

Adding suffixes to words ending with *y*

To add **ing** when a word ends with **y**, just add it!

  try trying

But, to add any other suffixes, first change the **y** to **i** before adding the suffix:

  try tried   messy messily

1 Add *ing* and *ed* to these words:

  cry dry fry fly spy

2 Add *ness* and *ly* to each of these words, and write the new words:

  happy sloppy stormy shifty

Use two of your new words in a sentence.

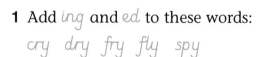

Remember

Conjunctions are sometimes called **joining words**. They are useful when we join short sentences.

Word work

● To learn the rule for adding suffixes to words ending with *y*

Remember

Spelling rules are very helpful, but they don't always work!

Word work

● To practise using tricky verbs

 Remember

Helper words are small words that help main verbs.

Using fell, drove, ran and fallen, driven, run

There is an easy way to remember when to use **fell**, **drove**, **ran** and when to use **fallen**, **driven**, **run**.
Never use a helping verb with fell, drove, ran:
The acorns fell from the tree.
Always use a helping verb like **had**, with fallen, driven, run:
The acorns had fallen from the tree.

1 Use the correct verb in these sentences:

  a *The shepherd had (drove/driven) his sheep up the hill.*

  b *One (ran/run) into the next valley.*

  c *Another had (fell/fallen) over a rock cliff.*

  d *Two (fell/fallen) into an old mine shaft.*

  e *The old man decided it was time he (drove/driven) them to a safer spot.*

  f *His dog (ran/run) to keep the flock together.*

2 Make up a sentence using both *fell* and *fallen*.

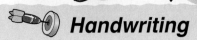 **Handwriting**   ## Letter spacing

The old shepherd was planting oak trees.

 1 Write the sentence three times. Try to make it even neater each time. Think carefully about the space between each word – not too wide, not too narrow.

2 Copy two or three sentences from a piece of work you have recently written. Write them as neatly as possible, thinking especially about the spacing between the words.

The Train to Glasgow

Double negatives

- To avoid using double negatives in sentences

Remember, if there are two negative words in one sentence, they can sometimes cancel each other out.
A negative sentence then becomes positive.

> I won't not catch that train!

Think about it. This means that Donald **will** catch his train.

1 Correct each of these negative sentences, so that they mean what the writer really intended.

 a "You've not got no chance of catching that train, Donald," shouted the ticket man.

 b "I couldn't get up no earlier, I was too tired," said Donald.

 c "I didn't have no breakfast," said Donald, pathetically.

 d "This train won't never wait for you again," said the guard, crossly.

 e "I promise I'll not be late never again," said Donald.

2 a Write these sentences, putting *anything* or *nothing* in the gaps:

 His mum couldn't do _____ to get him up any earlier. There was _____ his dad could do either.

 b Write two sentences, one using *anything* and one using *nothing*

Sentence work

- To practise apostrophes for possession in plural nouns

Word work

- To become increasingly aware of silent letters

Tip
Use a dictionary to help you.

Who owns it?

> *Donald's case*
>
> Remember, when something belongs to someone we use an apostrophe (') and an *s*, like this: *'s*.
>
> **Donald's** is called a **possessive noun**.
>
> For plurals of nouns ending with *s*, like *boys*, we put an apostrophe after the *s*: *The two boys' cases.*
>
> For plurals of nouns that don't end with *s*, like men, we add *'s*: *The men's cases.*

1 Write these using possessive nouns:

    a the newspapers belonging to the men

    b the sweets the children are eating

    c the carriage the team is travelling in

    d the patience the crowd is showing

2 Copy each phrase, adding an apostrophe in the correct place:

    a *the two childrens crisps*

    b *the three womens books*

    c *the three bands drummer*

    d *the two girls books*

Silent letters

> *Here is the guard from Donibristle.*
>
> Some words don't make a sound when read, like *u* in guard and *t* in Donibristle.

1 These words look wrong. All the **silent** letters have been left out. Copy the words, adding the missing letters.

    thisle thistle   gard lisen tonge clim thum
    onestly reumatism wispering gost anser reckage

2 Copy each word. Circle the silent letter. Write sentences using three of the words.

    wrench resign designer gnat wrapped
    tomb plumbing wrath rhyme

Using there, their, there's and theirs

Their cases are over <u>there</u>. The big ones are <u>theirs</u>, so <u>there's</u> no way they will catch <u>their</u> train without my help.

- **there** usually means *a place*
- **there's** is a contraction for *there is*
- **their** and **theirs** mean *belonging to people*

Word work

- To learn to use *there, their, there's* and *theirs*

Remember

A contraction is a short way of writing two words.

1 Choose *there* or *their* to fill each gap:

a "Your platform is over _____," said the porter.

b The family ran, carrying _____ luggage.

c "Will _____ be long to wait?" asks the girl.

d _____ bus had been late getting to the station.

2 Choose *there's* or *theirs* to fill each gap:

a "_____ no time to buy sweets," said Dad.

b Dad told the lady the seats were _____.

c "Look, _____ a ticket on them saying they are reserved," he told her.

d "_____ a spare seat over there for you," said Mum to the lady.

ere and *eir* patterns

Handwriting

ere eir ere eir ere eir ere eir ere eir ere eir

1 a Practise the letter patterns three times.
  b Neatly copy the words twice each:

here there were where
heir their theirs weir weird

2 Neatly copy the silly sentence:

They love to travel here, there and everywhere.

Morag and the Monster

Sentence work

- To practise recognising and using prepositions

Tip

Prepositions are always used with a noun or pronoun e.g.
above the water
among the ripples.

Remember

A **pronoun** stands in place of a noun.

Prepositions

The dark spot rose _above_ the water … _among_ the ripples.

Prepositions tell us the **position** of something compared with something else.

1 Copy these sentences. Circle the preposition and underline the noun or pronoun it is referring to.

  a Morag lives in Scotland.

  b Somewhere among them a child's voice shrieked.

  c It raised a great flurry of water behind it.

  d The sun struck sparkles of light from the greyish humps.

  e Now it looked black against the sun.

2 Write sentences about the picture using these prepositional phrases. When you have finished, underline the prepositions.

  a in the loch

  b on the beach

  c from the hill

  d through the water

Practising punctuation

1 Copy these sentences, adding the missing capital letters and punctuation:

a morag a young scottish girl had always wanted to see the loch ness monster

b her parents had brought her to the loch when she was three four five and seven years old and now she is nine she is back again

c they had heard that mr mackenzie had seen some unusual ripples on tuesday as he was driving past the loch on his way home from work

2 Copy these sentences, adding the missing capital letters and speech punctuation:

a please let's go to the loch to see if we can see nessie pleaded the girl persistently

b fine replied her father but i'm not sitting around all day looking at the loch like we did on wednesday

c the girl sat watching the ripples and then with an excited shriek she shouted the monster it's the loch ness monster

Dictionary practice

1 Use your dictionary to correct these words, all of which are spelt incorrectly:

apeared   rippels   paches   voise   shreaked
direcshun   digonal   sparckles   altored
parralel   dissapointment   dissapeared

2 Write your own definition of each of the bold words, and then write the dictionary definition:

a **diagonal** line   **parallel** lines   a **ripple**

Sentence work

● To revise the punctuation of longer, more complicated sentences, including speech

Remember

Commas should be used in **lists**, and where you want the reader to make a **brief pause**.

Word work

● To practise using a dictionary to check spellings

65

Word work

● To learn when to use who and whom

Using who and whom

> Morag is a girl <u>who</u> is sure the Loch Ness Monster is very real.
>
> Morag is a girl <u>to</u> <u>whom</u> the Loch Ness Monster is very real.
>
> preposition

Who changes to **whom** after a preposition.

1 Add *who* or *whom* to each of these sentences:

a _____ believes in the Loch Ness Monster?

b The man to _____ I spoke said that he did.

c He is someone for _____ I have the greatest respect.

d He told me his father, _____ is now over eighty, is a great 'Nessie' fan.

e It was thanks to his father, from _____ he had caught his great enthusiasm, that he was watching for the monster now.

2 Add two more sentences about Morag and the Monster, one using **who** and the other using **whom**.

 Handwriting

wh patterns

> wha whe whi who why wha whe whi who why

1 a Practise the letter patterns three times.

b Neatly copy these words twice each:

what whatever when where whether
white which while who
whom whose whole why

2 Neatly write all of the small words that you can find in each of these words:

white   whatever   whether   nowhere

Stop the Airport!

Using the simple present tense

Sentence work

- To practise writing formally

> The airport management believes a new terminal is important, whereas the local people think it is unnecessary.

When describing different sides in an argument, we normally use present tense verbs (e.g. **believes**, **think**), and try not to use too many personal pronouns.

Remember

Personal pronouns are used in place of people's names e.g. *we I they he she them.*

1 Rewrite these past tense sentences in the present tense. The first is done for you.

a They thought a new terminal would mean more planes.

They think a new terminal means more planes.

b She said fumes made her choke.

c The man from the airport said that the new planes were quieter and cleaner.

d They believed there should have been a public meeting about the new development.

2 Rewrite this paragraph, making it more *formal* and less *chatty*. Use present tense verbs and remove as many personal pronouns as possible.

My friends and I at our school hope that the new terminal won't be built, well at least not while we go to the school. Our school was extended not long ago and it would be a terrible waste for it all to be knocked down now, just after we moved into our lovely new buildings that we like so much. But we know the airport needs a new terminal if some airlines are not to move away to other airports.

Sentence work

- To learn about setting out a formal letter

Remember

1 Your address must be at the top, so that the person can reply.

2 The date you are writing.

3 The person you are writing to, and his or her address.

4 Use Sir and Madam if you don't know their name.

5 The message should be short and not too chatty.

6 Use **Yours faithfully**, if you wrote to Dear Sir or Madam, but **Yours sincerely**, if you know the person's name.

Writing formal letters

1 St Mary's School
Hall Road
Brentfield
BD13 6SR

2 18th May

3 The General Manager
Birmchester Airport
Brentfield
BD2 5GT

4 Dear Sir or Madam

5 We are aware that the airport management is intending to ...

Formal letters are set out differently from letters to friends.

1 Set out the beginning and end of a letter from your home address to the mayor of your city or town.

2 Set out the beginning and end of a letter from your school address to your Member of Parliament. Try to find out the correct address of the Houses of Parliament.

Changing verbs to nouns

Some nouns are made by adding a suffix to a verb e.g.

improve improve*ment*   operate opera*tion*

1 Copy and finish this table.

Verb	Noun	Verb	Noun	Verb	Noun
agree	agreement	depart	departure	discuss	discussion
enjoy		press		express	
replace		fail		depress	
involve		please		pollute	

2 Use a dictionary to check the spellings of all the words you have made in the table.

Word work

- To use suffixes to change verbs to nouns

Remember

Abstract nouns are names of feelings, emotions, actions, qualities etc., that we can't see or touch.

Using doesn't and don't

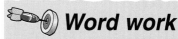

> *He <u>doesn't</u> want the new terminal.*
>
> **Doesn't** is the contraction of **does not**. Use it with singular nouns and pronouns *he, she, it.*
>
> *We <u>don't</u> want the new terminal.*
>
> **Don't** is the contraction of **do not**. Use it with plural nouns and the pronouns *I, you, we, they.*

Word work

● To practise using the two contractions *doesn't* and *don't*

1 Choose *doesn't* or *don't* to go with each of these pronouns:

She _____ They _____ He _____ I _____
We _____ It _____ You _____

2 Use the correct contraction in each sentence:

a *I <u>doesn't/don't</u> know why they need a new building.*

b *We <u>doesn't/don't</u> want all the extra planes that will be flying over our town.*

c *<u>Doesn't/Don't</u> this placard belong to you, James?*

d *It <u>doesn't/don't</u> matter whether the planes are quieter, we'll still get the fumes.*

e *They <u>doesn't/don't</u> seem prepared to listen to us.*

f *That new manager <u>doesn't/don't</u> care what we all think.*

ness and *ment* patterns

Handwriting

> *ness ment ness ment ness ment ness ment*

1 a Practise the letter patterns three times.
   b Neatly copy the words twice each:

> *laziness ugliness nastiness emptiness*
> *treatment department entertainment compartment*

2 Write three sentences, each of which includes at least one **ness** or **ment** word.

Almaz

 Sentence work

● To revise word classes

 Tip

Different types of words are sometimes called **parts of speech**.

The word machine

We have learnt about different types of words.

Nouns are naming words.

Pronouns are used in place of nouns.

Adjectives describe nouns.

Verbs are action or being words.

Adverbs usually describe verbs.

Conjunctions are joining words.

Prepositions describe position.

1 Write each of these words in a sentence. Say which part of speech each is in your sentences.

girl watched in she sadly young and

2 Read these sentences. Copy the chart and write the words in the boxes to which they belong.

The young girl's father called her over and spoke to her. He talked quietly but firmly.

Noun	Pronoun	Adjective	
Verb	Adverb	Conjunction	Preposition

Practising dialogue

1 Copy each of these sentences, adding the missing speech marks and commas:

   a I am going to get married again said Almaz's father.

   b My new wife is quite young said her father and I hope you will like her.

   c Almaz said to her friend I don't want a new stepmother that I have to respect and obey.

   d You will soon get to like her said the friend.

2 Rewrite this short paragraph, starting a new line when a different person begins to speak, and adding the missing speech marks and commas:

I miss my mother dreadfully said Almaz to her father. I know you do replied her father. I don't want a new mother said Almaz. Kibret is going to be my new wife said her father so you must treat her as your mother. But said Almaz sadly she can never replace my own dear mother who died.

Changing nouns to verbs

> As many abstract nouns are made by adding a suffix to a verb, many verbs are made by taking away suffixes e.g.
>
> improve*ment*   improve
> opera*tion*   operate

1 Copy and finish this table.

Noun	Verb	Noun	Verb	Noun	Verb
encouragement	encourage	departure	depart	sensation	sense
enjoyment		pleasure		completion	
entertainment		failure		attraction	
attachment		pressure		satisfaction	

2 Use a dictionary to check the spellings of all the words you have made in the table.

Sentence work

● To revise the punctuation of dialogue

Remember

Dialogue is spoken words and sentences.

Word work

● To change nouns to verbs by taking away suffixes

Remember

Abstract nouns are names of feelings, emotions, actions, qualities etc., that we can't see or touch.

Sentence work

● To revise idioms

Idioms

> *Almaz's father was the sort of person to <u>call a spade a spade</u>.*

Remember, **an idiom** is an expression that has a meaning different from the usual meaning of the individual words within it.

1 Write in your own words what you think each of these idioms means:

  a Almaz's father was never likely to **beat about the bush**.

  b Almaz looked at Kibret and **tried to catch her eye**.

  c She wanted to **bury the hatchet** with Kibret.

2 Put each of these idioms in a sentence:

  smell a rat   skating on thin ice
  over the moon   keep something dark

Handwriting

ion, *sion* and *tion* patterns

> *ion sion tion ion sion tion ion sion tion*

1 a Practise the letter patterns three times.
  b Neatly copy these words twice each:

  champion suspicion million fashion
  attraction reaction definition examination
  decision discussion possession occasion

2 Look through some books and find, and write neatly, three more *tion* words and three more *sion* words.